I0569331

Rhythms of War

The Teen Warrior Series: Drummer Boys of the Civil War
History's battles weren't just fought by grown men.

Discover the incredible true stories of the youngest
on the front lines: the drummer boys. Too young
to fight, yet too brave to stay home, these boys
marched into danger with nothing but a drum—and
unshakable courage.

Explore how they lived, what they endured, and
why their role was so vital.

Meet real kids who braved cannon fire, inspired
soldiers, and beat out commands that changed the
tides of battles. Along the way, you'll find hands-
on activities, creative projects, and fascinating
glimpses into camp life, communication, and
courage under fire.

Part history. Part heart. All true.

Perfect for curious minds ages 11–14

KM BOOKS

Kellie May

Edited by Nicola Rooney

Content

Author's Note and Disclaimer

On Balance, Perspective, and Historical Records

This book—and those that follow—contain more stories, details, and first-hand accounts from the Union side of the American Civil War than the Confederate. This is not meant to cast judgment or to demonize Confederate soldiers or civilians. Rather, it reflects a practical reality of historical research: **far more records, memoirs, and personal stories from the Union side have survived, been published, and made accessible.**

As with many conflicts throughout history, the side that emerges victorious often shapes the historical narrative. The Union's greater literacy rates, publishing access, and post-war preservation efforts have contributed to this imbalance.

Where reliable accounts from Confederate perspectives exist— especially those of drummer boys or child participants—they are included with care and respect. The goal of this book is to honor the humanity, hardship, and courage shown by young people on both sides of the war.

History is complex. These books aim to illuminate it, not simplify it.

Introduction to The Teen Warrior Series

War is often told through the stories of grown men—soldiers, generals, and presidents. But history has another voice: the voice of young people who stood up, stepped forward, and helped shape the course of a nation.

Across the battlefields of the Revolutionary and Civil Wars, young people played critical roles. Boys worked as messengers, scouts, water bearers, and even spies. Girls ran farms, raised siblings, nursed the wounded, and sometimes disguised themselves to fight. These weren't side characters— they were **warriors** and **patriots** in their own right.

Over the course of this first series, you'll meet brave teens— boys and girls—who played powerful roles in the **Civil War**. Then, in **The Teen Patriot Series**, we'll step back in time to the **Revolutionary War**, where a new generation of young heroes fought for freedom in a very different America.

Each book blends fact with fiction, helping you step into the shoes of real young people who faced danger, made tough choices, and helped make history.

The Teen Warrior Series begins here with the true story of the **drummer boys** of the Civil War—some as young as nine—who marched alongside soldiers, braved battlefields, and carried more than drums. They carried courage. Their drumbeats signaled commands, lifted spirits, and kept troops moving through the chaos of war. But they were just one part of a much larger story.

This first book lays the groundwork. You'll learn what a drummer boy was, how he lived, what he did, and why he mattered. But this is only the beginning.

These were not just kids. They were warriors.

And their stories are waiting to be told.

Children at War:
The Many Roles of Young Patriots

Before we march beside the drummer boys, it's important to understand the full army of young people who fought wars without necessarily carrying a musket.

In the Revolutionary and Civil Wars, children found themselves pulled into the heart of conflict. Boys too young to enlist sometimes joined as messengers, racing between commanders under cannon fire. Their small size and speed made them ideal for slipping through enemy lines unnoticed. Others became scouts, sneaking ahead of troops to gather information about enemy positions—a dangerous task that required nerves of steel.

Some boys worked as water bearers, sprinting across battlefields with heavy canteens to keep soldiers alive under the blistering sun. Others, barely teenagers, became unofficial aides to officers, carrying supplies, tending to wounded horses, and helping maintain order when chaos reigned.

Girls fought their own battles, often just as dangerous. When fathers and brothers marched off to war, daughters stayed behind to manage farms and protect their families. Some disguised themselves as boys to enlist, risking death not only from bullets but also from discovery. Others nursed the wounded in field hospitals, facing disease and heartbreak daily, while a few even acted as spies, slipping secret information past enemy guards with bravery far beyond their years.

The wars of the eighteenth and nineteenth centuries were fought not just by soldiers in uniform but by a whole generation of young people—children who rose to the moment with a courage few could imagine.

Among them, the drummer boys stood apart: their role was unique, their bravery undeniable, and their beat echoed across history.

Now, let's step closer. Let's meet the boys who carried the heart of the army in their hands—and paid a heavy price for it.

□ Vocabulary Box	
Word	**Definition**
Snare Drum	A small drum with strings under the bottom that makes a sharp, rattling sound
Drummer Boy	A young boy who played drum signals to guide soldiers during war
Bass Drum	A large drum with a deep sound
Fife	A small, high-pitched flute used in military bands
Morale	The confidence or spirit of a group, especially during tough times
Retreat	To move back or withdraw from battle

Timeline of Drummer Boys in History

1. American Revolution (1775–1783)

o Drummer boys played a key role in military communication, helping to signal orders and maintain morale among soldiers.

o They also helped with camp duties, such as delivering messages and supplies.

2. War of 1812 (1812–1815)

o Drummer boys continued to be essential for communication during battles and helped maintain order in chaotic situations.

o They were often positioned at the front lines with the officers to keep the rhythm of marching and signaling.

3. American Civil War (1861–1865)

o Drummer boys were especially prominent, often marching with soldiers and serving as part of military bands.

o They played a crucial role in battlefield communication, with different drumbeats signaling orders like **advance** or **retreat**.

4. World War I (1914–1918)

o The role of drummer boys diminished significantly due to technological advancements in communication (like radios) and the shift to larger, more mechanized armies.

o However, military bands still used drums to boost morale and maintain rhythm in marching units.

o Drummer boys were no longer a primary component on the battlefield but were still present in military bands and ceremonial functions.

5. Post-World War I (1920s Onward)

o Drummer boys transitioned out of active military roles, but their legacy continues in military bands, marching bands, and ceremonial duties.

o The role became more symbolic, with drummer boys seen in parades, memorial events, and historical reenactments.

Rhythms of War: Drummer Boys of the Revolutionary and Civil Wars

Long ago, in a land built on freedom and courage, two great wars shaped the future of a nation. The Revolutionary War and the Civil War were not just battles of soldiers and weapons but of ideas and beliefs that clashed across fields, valleys, and hills.

Amid the roar of cannons and the crack of muskets, there were heroes whose names never made it into history books. Among them were the drummer boys—young, fearless, and vital to the fight. Their rhythms guided armies, lifted spirits, and echoed through the chaos of war. This is their story.

Meet "Lil Gib"— The 79th Ohio Infantry's 10-Year-Old Drummer Boy!

Carte de Visite by Joseph H. **Van Stavoren of Nashville, Tenn.** Rick Carlile Collection.

Imagine being just 10 years old and marching alongside soldiers in the Civil War! That's what Gilbert VanZant—nicknamed "Lil Gib" by his fellow soldiers—did. He was the 79th Ohio Infantry's drummer boy, and this photo captures him proudly standing with his drum in Nashville, Tennessee, around 1863 or 1864.

Look at his uniform—it's not just an ordinary outfit! His jacket has fancy curls and a unique cuff design, showing that even drummer boys had their own style on the battlefield. His drumbeats helped keep the troops in step and boosted their spirits during tough times.

The Call of the Drums

Imagine stepping into the shoes of a twelve-year-old boy during the **Revolutionary War**. The air hums with excitement and tension as soldiers ready themselves for battle. Amid the chaos, a steady, rhythmic drumbeat rises above the noise, signaling the start of something monumental.

Drummer boys played a vital role in these historic wars. Their job was far more than just keeping a beat; they were the heartbeat of the army, relaying critical commands through the language of drumming. With each roll and tap, they signaled orders like "Advance," "Retreat," or "Prepare to Fire." On the battlefield, where shouts were drowned out by cannon fire and musket shots, the drum was a soldier's guide—a lifeline in the midst of war.

The Young Patriots

Many drummer boys in the **Revolutionary War** were barely teenagers, yet their courage stood tall. These young patriots faced the challenges of war head-on, inspiring soldiers and civilians alike. The beat of their drums wasn't just a rhythm; it was a symbol of resilience and determination. Esther Forbes wrote a famous novel about a fictional drummer boy called "Johnny Tremaine."

A Symphony of Unity

The drummer boys' roles changed between the two wars. During the **Revolutionary War**, drummer boys primarily served to relay orders and maintain communication, keeping soldiers in sync with the battle's rhythm.

In contrast, drummer boys like Orion Howe became more symbolic of unity and morale during the **Civil War**. While still aiding in communication, they also provided a psychological boost for soldiers, helping them stay focused amid the turmoil of war. Their presence in the Civil War highlighted a stronger emotional connection to the soldiers' perseverance through adversity.

Orion Howe, who joined the Union Army at the tender age of thirteen, faced unimaginable challenges. The beat of his drum echoed through the chaos of the battlefield, providing a steady rhythm for soldiers marching into the unknown.

The Young Drummer Boys:
Heroes in the Making

During the **Revolutionary War** and the **Civil War**, drummer boys were often incredibly young, typically ranging from just **9 or 10 years old** to their mid-teens. Most of them were between **12 and 14**, small enough to maneuver quickly through the ranks yet tough enough to handle the challenges of war.

But why were such young boys chosen for such a vital role? The military believed younger drummers were more agile and could keep up with the fast pace of marching. Their smaller size made it easier for them to navigate through the battlefield and around the soldiers. Plus, they were thought to be more resilient to the harsh conditions of war.

Despite their age, these boys were essential to military operations.

They used their drums to relay commands and orders, keeping the troops in sync. The drummer boys endured the same dangers as the adult soldiers and displayed extraordinary courage. Some even became legends, celebrated for their bravery and inspiring the soldiers around them. These young heroes were more than just the rhythm of the battlefield—they were symbols of determination and spirit.

Drummer Boy Uniforms in the Revolutionary and Civil Wars

Drummer boys during the **Revolutionary** and **Civil War**s wore uniforms that were generally similar to those of the soldiers in their respective armies. While there could be variations based on units or regions, here is an overview of their typical attire:

Revolutionary War (1775-1783)

1. **Coat**: A long coat, usually made of wool or wool blends in regimental colors or standard uniform of the unit

2. **Breeches**: Knee-length breeches, typically made of wool, fastened with buttons, providing comfort for marching

3. **Waistcoat (Vest)**: A waistcoat or vest worn over a shirt and under the coat, made from a fabric matching the coat

4. **Shirt**: A long-sleeved, linen or cotton shirt worn under the waistcoat for added warmth and comfort

5. **Stockings**: Knee-high stockings made from wool, often worn with garters to keep them in place

6. **Shoes**: Leather shoes, usually with buckles, built for durability during long marches

7. **Tricorn Hat**: The iconic three-cornered hat, a distinguishing feature of Revolutionary War military attire

8. **Drum Carriage**: A leather or fabric sling designed to carry the drum over the shoulder, allowing freedom of movement

Civil War (1861-1865)

1. **Frock Coat**: A wool frock coat, often extending below the waist, with color and style depending on the regiment

2. **Trousers**: Wool trousers matching the frock coat, frequently adorned with a stripe down the sides to identify the unit

3. **Vest**: A wool vest worn under the frock coat and over the shirt, providing extra warmth

4. **Shirt**: A long-sleeved cotton or linen shirt worn under the vest for comfort

5. **Stockings**: Woolen stockings similar to those worn in the Revolutionary War, often held up with suspenders

6. **Brogans**: Leather ankle boots or brogans, sturdy enough for long marches and daily wear

7. **Kepi or Forage Cap**: A kepi (military cap) or forage cap with a brim, typically adorned with regimental insignia

8. **Drum Carriage**: Like the Revolutionary War, a sling or strap to carry the drum over the shoulder

These uniforms were designed for practicality, offering warmth, mobility, and durability. While the exact details varied by unit and availability of materials, they were crafted to serve functional and identification purposes on the battlefield. Drummer boys dressed in these uniforms stood out for their role and the distinctive attire that made them easily recognizable among the troops.

Drumbeats on Both Sides: Union vs. Confederate Drummer Boys

During the Civil War, the battlefield pulsed with the rhythms of war, and drummer boys were at the heart of that beat. North or South, these young musicians played more than just music; they carried commands, rallied spirits, and grew up far too quickly.

What They Had in Common

__**Young and Eager** Most drummer boys were just 12 to 16 years old. Swept up by the adventure and purpose of war, many enlisted with dreams of glory, often hiding their real age.

__ **Tough Conditions** Mud, hunger, fear, and freezing nights—drummer boys endured the same hardships as soldiers. They marched, camped, and bled alongside their regiments.

__ **Drummers, Not Just Musicians**
Their rhythms signaled troop movements, battle commands, and daily routines. A drumbeat could mean "advance," "retreat," or "hold the line." In chaos, it was order.

__ **Bravery Beyond Their Years**
Some ran into fire to retrieve flags; others stood firm under cannon blasts. Their courage didn't go unnoticed—many received medals or commendations.

How Their Worlds Differed

__ Gear and Supplies

Union drummer boys often had regulation drums and uniforms. Confederates? Not so lucky. Scarce supplies meant homemade drums and mismatched outfits.

__ Who Got Drafted

Union drummer boys were usually volunteers. In the South, dwindling manpower meant even younger boys were sometimes pressed into service.

__ Uniforms in Contrast

Northern boys had more consistent attire thanks to better manufacturing. Southern boys often wore a patchwork of military and civilian clothing.

__ Culture and Identity

Drummer boys in the North came from cities, farms, and immigrant families. Southern boys were steeped in regional traditions and a deeply rooted way of life.

Shoot the first Man that attempts
to pull down the American Flag.

Dressed for Duty:
A Union Drummer Boy's Uniform

A Union drummer boy's uniform during the Civil War closely resembled that of regular infantrymen, but with distinct touches that set these young musicians apart. The uniform, designed for practicality and symbolism, reflected the regulations of the era while acknowledging the drummer boys' unique role on the battlefield. Here's a breakdown of what a Union drummer boy typically wore:

1. **Jacket:** A short, dark blue wool jacket, often styled like the infantry frock coat. Drummer boys sometimes wore decorative trim or small embellishments to mark their special role.

2. **Trousers:** Sky-blue wool trousers were built to endure rough conditions in camp and on the march.

3. **Kepi or Forage Cap:** A kepi (a stiff, flat-topped cap) or a forage cap with a softer crown. Both were dark blue and featured insignia or piping indicating the regiment.

4. **Shirt and Necktie:** A cotton or wool shirt beneath the jacket. A cravat or necktie, occasionally in red or another contrasting color, was a common accessory.

5. **Drum Sling:** A wide leather sling worn diagonally over the shoulder held the drum securely in front. This allowed the drummer to play while marching or standing to attention.

6. **Drummer's Sword:** Some drummer boys carried a ceremonial short sword, symbolizing their official role in the army.

7. **Shoes:** Sturdy leather brogans or ankle boots helped them keep pace during long marches.

Gray Beats and Southern Threads: The Confederate Drummer Boy's Uniform

During the Civil War, Confederate drummer boys dressed a lot like regular soldiers, but their uniforms were less consistent. Because the South had fewer supplies, their clothing often depended on what was available in their area, or even from home. Here's a quick look at what they usually wore:

1. **Jacket or Frock Coat:** Due to dye shortages, a dark gray single-breasted jacket or frock coat, sometimes tinged with "butternut" brown. Jacket styles varied by regiment. Any embellishments were modest and rare.

2. **Trousers:** Trousers made of wool or homespun fabric typically matched the jacket in gray or butternut shades. Durability, not uniformity, was the priority.

3. **Kepi or Slouch Hat:** Confederate drummer boys often wore either a kepi—a soft, flat-topped cap—or a slouch hat with a broad brim. These were fashioned from wool or felt, sometimes adorned with minimal insignia.

4. **Shirt and Necktie:** Beneath their jackets, boys wore cotton or homespun shirts, sometimes accompanied by a simple cravat or necktie. Patterns were plain and practical, reflecting what was available at the time.

5. **Drum Sling:** A leather or canvas drum sling over their shoulders allowed them to play while marching. These were often handmade or repurposed from available materials.

6. **Shoes:** Footwear ranged from military-issue leather brogans to civilian shoes, depending on what could be scrounged or supplied.

7. **Non-Combatant Sword or Knife:** While not intended for battle, some drummer boys were issued small ceremonial swords or knives—symbols of their honorary status within the ranks.

8. **Rank Insignia:** Though rare, some Confederate drummer boys displayed rank insignia on sleeves or caps, reflecting their standing within the regiment.

What Drove Children to Join?

When the Civil War began, it wasn't just the sound of cannons or the marching of boots that stirred the hearts of the nation—it was the call to duty, to adventure, to something bigger than oneself. And children heard it, too.

In towns across the country, the war didn't only arrive through newspapers but in everyday places: blacksmith shops, church pews, and kitchen tables. People spoke of patriotism and sacrifice. Parades filled with flags and music passed through dusty main streets. Drums pounded, fifes whistled, and banners waved. Boys watched their older brothers and neighbors step forward to serve, and many felt the same pull.

Some were driven by a deep love of country. Others were eager for the excitement, the chance to see the world beyond their town. A few simply wanted to be near a father or older brother already in uniform. Whatever the reason, these boys didn't wait to grow up— they acted.

They lied about their age, borrowed clothes to look older, or snuck onto wagons as units rolled out. They trained, marched, played drums, and faced the same dangers as the men beside them.

These weren't just childhood dreams. They were brave choices made in a time of national crisis, and they left behind stories of courage that still echo today.

Creative Ways Drummer Boys Enlisted

Eager to contribute to the war effort, many young boys went to great lengths to enlist in the Revolutionary and Civil Wars. Their determination and resourcefulness sometimes led them to use creative and daring tactics to join the army, often bypassing age restrictions or other enlistment requirements. Despite their initial deception, many of these boys became symbols of bravery and were integral to the war effort.

Here are some examples of how these young drummer boys enlisted:

1. Falsifying Age
Many drummer boys lied about their age to meet the enlistment requirements. They forged documents or misled recruiters, claiming to be older than they were.

2. Running Away
Running away from home was a common way for boys to enlist in the army. They were driven by a sense of duty, a yearning for independence, or even a desire to escape difficult home lives. This tactic was risky, as joining without parental consent was illegal.

3. Disguises
A few drummer boys disguised themselves to appear older. They wore oversized clothing or even attempted to grow facial hair. These disguises allowed them to fool recruiters and enlist under false pretenses.

4. Assuming False Identities
Some boys assumed false identities. They took on different names or claimed to be someone else entirely, hoping their real age and background would go unnoticed. This tactic made it difficult for recruiters to verify their true identities, allowing them to enlist without question.

5. Bribing Recruiters
In certain instances, young drummer boys resorted to bribing recruiters. They offered money or valuables to influence the recruiter's decision and bypass age restrictions. With military units desperate to meet enlistment quotas, some recruiters were willing to overlook the age requirements in exchange for bribes.

The Vital Role of Drummer Boys

Drummer boys played a crucial role in wars like the Revolutionary War and the Civil War for several important reasons:

In the heat of battle, with smoke and confusion all around, it was essential for soldiers to **identify their units**. Each regiment or battalion had its own distinctive drumbeat, helping soldiers recognize their comrades and maintain formation. This was crucial for preventing friendly fire and ensuring the effectiveness of military strategies.

Communication was challenging during battles. The sounds of musket fire, cannons, and general chaos made it difficult for soldiers to hear verbal commands. Drummer boys used the rhythmic beats of their drums to convey essential commands to the troops. Each beat had a specific meaning that helped coordinate the movements of large groups of soldiers.

Drummer boys sometimes had additional responsibilities, including helping the wounded. Their steady presence on the battlefield meant they could quickly relay messages for **medical assistance** or carry water to injured soldiers.

The presence of young drummer boys was a **powerful symbol of patriotism and sacrifice**. Their bravery in the face of danger inspired soldiers and civilians, highlighting that everyone, regardless of age, had a role to play in the fight for freedom.

War is a frightening and intense experience, especially for young soldiers. The presence of drummer boys on the battlefield served as a **source of inspiration and motivation**. The steady beat of the drums created a sense of order and purpose, boosting the troops' morale and reminding them that they were part of a unified force.

The drummers represented **discipline** and order within the army. The rhythmic sound of the drums created a sense of structure and control, even in the chaotic environment of war. This discipline was essential for maintaining the integrity of military formations and strategies.

The Many Roles of Drummer Boys: More Than Just Drums

While drummer boys are often remembered for their musical duties, they were also essential to the day-to-day functioning of the military. These young heroes were expected to pitch in and take on various tasks beyond playing their drums—they were vital to the success of their units.

1. Medical Assistants

Drummer boys often helped the regimental surgeons and medical teams. Their agility allowed them to swiftly move through the ranks, assisting with the care of wounded soldiers.

2. Water Carriers

During marches and on the battlefield, drummer boys were sometimes tasked with carrying water to the troops—an essential job, especially under the scorching heat of battle.

3. Orderly Duties

They assisted officers, running messages, delivering orders, and handling errands to keep the military unit running smoothly.

4. Equipment Maintenance

Drummer boys helped maintain the equipment, from cleaning muskets to caring for their drums and other essential gear.

5. Camp Chores

Like all soldiers, drummer boys were part of camp life, helping to set up camp, cook, and generally keep the unit functioning.

6. Messenger and Communication

They frequently acted as messengers, carrying orders between units or delivering important communications on the battlefield.

7. Guard Duty

Some drummer boys were assigned guard duty, helping maintain security around the camp and keeping watch at night.

8. Training and Drill Assistance

They also assisted in military training and drills, helping soldiers practice commands and keeping the beat during practice sessions.

The Dangers of Being a Drummer Boy

Being a drummer boy during the Revolutionary and Civil Wars was no easy task. These young boys faced the same dangers and hardships as adult soldiers, even though they weren't directly engaged in combat. Their role on the battlefield was fraught with risks and difficulties. Here are some of the challenges they faced:

1. Battlefield Dangers
Drummer boys didn't just march in parades; they were often right in the thick of the action, close to the front lines, positioned near officers to relay commands, exposed to gunfire, artillery, and the chaos of battle. Drummer boys didn't carry rifles but faced many of the same life-threatening dangers as soldiers; the only difference was that they couldn't defend themselves.

2. Wounded in Action
Some drummer boys were hit by stray bullets or flying debris while doing their job. Others took on the extra role of helping stretcher-bearers or comforting the wounded. They rushed into smoky chaos to give water, bandages, or a steadying hand. Doing this under fire took incredible courage.

3. Capture and Mistreatment
If captured by the enemy, drummer boys faced the same risk of mistreatment as adult prisoners of war. Being young didn't protect them from the harsh realities of captivity. They were marched to prison camps and exposed to the same hunger, illness, and fear faced by grown men. Some were released early, but others endured long months behind enemy lines.

What Drummer Boys Endured Daily

1. Exposure to Harsh Conditions

Like all soldiers, drummer boys had to endure harsh conditions.

Extreme weather, lack of proper clothing, and poor shelter were common, especially during long marches or prolonged campaigns. Whether it was summer's heat or winter's biting cold, drummer boys marched alongside soldiers through it all. They often slept under the stars with little more than a thin blanket. Rain soaked their clothes, mud clung to their boots, and snow could freeze their fingers to their drumsticks. Even at rest, there was rarely comfort.

2. Disease and Illness

More soldiers died from disease than from battle—drummer boys were just as vulnerable. Camps were crowded and dirty. Drinking water was often polluted, and food could be spoiled or scarce. With no antibiotics or vaccines, diseases like dysentery, measles, and pneumonia spread quickly. Even a simple cold could become life-threatening.

3. Physical Strain

A snare drum might not seem heavy at first, but carrying it all day, then playing it while marching, took a toll. Drummer boys had to keep pace with the troops during marches and drills, making it a physically demanding job that required stamina and endurance. Sore shoulders, blistered feet, and aching backs were all part of the job.

The Hidden Dangers Drummer Boys Faced

In both the **Revolutionary** and **Civil** Wars, drummer boys held no weapons, but they stood in harm's way all the same. These children carried the sound of command across deafening chaos. Their drumbeats signaled troops to advance, retreat, reload, or regroup, making them crucial to battlefield communication.

And that made them dangerous.

Though not official combatants, drummer boys were often positioned close to officers and color bearers—prime targets for enemy fire. The rhythmic beat of a drum could cut through the smoke and confusion of war, guiding soldiers like a compass. Silencing that beat could unravel a regiment's coordination. Whether by chance or grim calculation, drummer boys fell. Some were caught in the crossfire. Others, standing boldly in open lines, became unintentional targets simply because of where they stood and what they carried.

While there's little evidence of widespread, deliberate targeting, enemies *knew* the value of the drum. And on a battlefield where sound meant command, even a child's instrument could draw fatal attention.

What the Drums Meant to the Soldiers

When you think of a battlefield, you might picture shouting and cannon fire. But listen closer, and you would hear something else: the steady beat of a drum.

Drums did more than signal commands. They were the heartbeat of the army.

During long marches, when soldiers were tired, sore, and hungry, the drum kept their feet moving. Each beat pushed them onward, step by step, mile after mile.

In the chaos of battle, when smoke filled the air and the world felt like it was falling apart, the drum helped soldiers find their way. It gave rhythm to their actions, telling them when to charge, when to fall back, and when to reload. It cut through the fear and confusion.

At night, around the campfires, drummer boys sometimes played softer songs. The beat reminded soldiers that they weren't alone— that they were part of something bigger—that even in the darkest moments, they still had each other.

The drum wasn't just an instrument.

It was hope.
It was courage.
It was home.

Personal Stories from the Front

Captain's Report on Drummer Boy Thomas Garland:
"I never saw a child stand so steady under fire."

Elijah Taft, Drummer boy, 14:
"It was scratched, stained, and dented—but it still played. Just like me."

Union Drummer William Bircher:
"I painted my initials inside the rim so no one could claim it was theirs. I was proud of that drum."

Union Soldier:
"It told us when to eat, march, and fight. Sometimes, I wondered if it knew more about our lives than we did."

Private Henry Moore:
"When I couldn't find the words, I'd just play. That's how I knew I was still alive."

A soldier wrote:
"After he fell, we made sure the drum got home. It felt wrong to leave it behind."

I Painted a Star on Mine for Luck
"Every time I played it, I looked down at that star and told myself I'd make it home."

Confederate drummer, 13:
"When the world exploded around me, I gripped my sticks and played. If I could drum, I wasn't afraid."

Benjamin "Drumbeat" Turner:
The Drummer Boy Who Fought for Freedom

During the **Revolutionary War**, a determined 13-year-old boy named **Benjamin "Drumbeat" Turner** set out to make his mark. Born in a small colonial town, Benjamin developed a love for the rhythms of the drum from an early age. Driven by a desire to contribute to the fight for independence, he enlisted in the **Continental Army**, ready to serve in any way he could.

Though most drummer boys stayed behind the front lines, Benjamin's fierce spirit and determination didn't let him stay in the background. His bravery caught the eye of his superiors, who soon recognized his potential to be more than just a musician.

During a critical battle, Benjamin's courage was put to the test. In the thick of the fighting, the commanding officer called out, "Drumbeat, can you handle a musket?" Without a second thought, Benjamin nodded. The officer showed him the basics of firing and reloading, and Benjamin was ready to fight. He instantly transformed from a drummer boy into a soldier.

As the battle raged on, Benjamin's drum hung from his side while a musket rested in his hands. When the time came, he joined the infantry, firing alongside the soldiers. His small size allowed him to move swiftly on the battlefield, and his drumming kept the troops in step, maintaining order amid the chaos.

Benjamin's dual role as a drummer and a fighter inspired the soldiers around him. The rhythm of his drum became a rallying cry for the troops, uniting them in the heat of battle. They admired his courage and saw in him the embodiment of the Revolutionary spirit—a young boy fighting for liberty alongside grown men.

The commanding officer, witnessing the young boy's bravery, praised him for his exceptional service. Benjamin Turner became a symbol of determination and patriotism.

After the war, Benjamin continued to inspire his community. He shared his stories with younger generations, teaching them about courage, unity, and the importance of standing up for what's right.

The Return of Samuel Thornton

At fifteen, Samuel Thornton wanted more than life on the family farm.

Inspired by stories of courage and justice, he set his sights on becoming a **Union** Army drummer boy.

His parents, Martha and Henry, were heartbroken. Samuel was their only child, and the idea of sending him off to battle was unbearable. They pleaded with him to stay, but Samuel's resolve was ironclad. In the early light of an autumn morning, drum slung over his shoulder, he walked away—toward war, toward purpose, and toward the unknown.

The villagers watched in silence, admiring his courage, mourning the loss of a boy who had grown up before their eyes.

Months turned into years. Letters stopped coming. There were rumors his regiment had suffered heavy losses, and many villagers believed Samuel was dead. Martha wore a black shawl. Henry worked the fields in silence.

But Samuel wasn't dead. He had become a thread in the fabric of the war, his drumming a constant through chaos and bloodshed. He saw friends fall, learned to read fear in the eyes of grown men, and kept drumming even when his hands trembled. In one fierce battle, when everything seemed lost, Samuel's steady rhythm rallied his unit, helping them regroup and push back.

He came home at nineteen.

The village gathered as word spread—Samuel was alive. His parents ran to meet him, tears spilling freely. But the boy who left had not come back. He stood taller, moved slower, and spoke less. His eyes held memories no one could touch.

Villagers cheered but fell silent when they saw his face. Martha hugged him tightly. Henry placed a hand on his shoulder. And though Samuel smiled, it didn't reach his eyes. The drum he once carried with pride now rested silently at his feet.

Samuel had kept his promise—he came home. But the war had changed him. Still, the village welcomed him with open arms, proud of the boy who had left and grateful for the man who returned.

Thomas "Tommy" Cooper:
The Youngest Drummer Boy of the Civil War

Born in a small village in the North, Tommy's journey would become a shining example of youthful courage in the face of war's unimaginable hardships.

At **nine years old**, Tommy's world was turned upside down when his older brother enlisted in the **Union** Army. Eager to stand by his brother's side and contribute to the cause, Tommy was determined to help. His unwavering spirit and innocence caught the eye of a compassionate officer, who, recognizing the boy's desire, allowed him to join as the regiment's drummer boy.

Tommy's drum, nearly as tall as he was, became an emblem of his commitment. The regiment, moved by his bravery, quickly took him under their wing. A smaller drum was specially made just for him, and Tommy became the **youngest drummer boy** in the Union Army.

Despite the hardships of war, Tommy's resilience never faltered.

Long marches, heavy gear, and the harsh conditions of military life tested his strength, but his determination never wavered. Seeing his grit and spirit, the soldiers came to admire and protect the young drummer boy.

During a crucial battle, as the sounds of musket fire and cannon blasts filled the air, Tommy's drumming provided a steady rhythm that kept the soldiers in formation. His small hands moved quickly and expertly over the drumhead, sending vital signals to the troops. Amid the chaos, Tommy's focus never wavered—he was more than just a boy with a drum; he was a beacon of courage.

After the battle, Tommy was seen helping the medics and offering water to the wounded. His selflessness and acts of kindness showed the true strength of character that defined him.

As news of Tommy's bravery spread, he became a symbol of hope and inspiration. His story, often shared in letters and newspapers, touched the hearts of people back home, showing them that even the youngest among them could make a monumental difference in times of war.

The Drummer Boy Who Ran to War

In the heart of Ohio, a spirited boy named Samuel "Sammy" Turner lived in a small farming town. Born in 1847, Sammy was no ordinary farm kid. He was inspired by the heroic stories told by soldiers returning from the front lines of the **Civil War**. His heart swelled with patriotism, and he dreamed of fighting for the **Union** cause. But there was just one problem—his parents were *completely* against it.

Sammy's mom and dad didn't want their son anywhere near the battlefield. They believed he was far too young and innocent to face the horrors of war. But Sammy didn't see it that way. The more he heard about the soldiers, the more determined he became to join them. He wasn't going to sit on the sidelines.

One quiet night in 1863, Sammy made up his mind. Under a silver moon in the dead of night, he packed a small bundle, slipped out of his family's farmhouse, and set off into the darkness. His heart pounded with excitement and fear as he tiptoed through the quiet streets of his town, careful not to wake anyone.

His destination? The nearby recruiting station. There, under the flickering campfire lights, he would do whatever it took to join the army. He told the recruiters he was older than his 15 years, giving them the age they wanted to hear. Without much hesitation, they accepted him into the Union Army. Sammy was in!

Now, instead of tending to crops and mucking out stables, Sammy was marching into history as a drummer boy. Through battles like Chickamauga and the Siege of Chattanooga, Sammy proved he was more than just a young boy with a dream—he was a fighter. Though small in stature, his bravery earned him the respect of soldiers many years older than him. But more than that, his youthful enthusiasm was contagious. He lifted the spirits of his comrades during the darkest times.

When the war ended and Sammy returned home, his parents were furious. But as they saw the young man standing before them, no longer the boy who ran away, they couldn't help but admire his courage. Sammy's adventure had turned him into a symbol of determination and bravery.

The Drummer Boy Who Lied to Fight

In New York City in 1848, Jamie Porter was born into a world brimming with energy, ambition, and patriotism. From the moment he could walk, the stories of courage and heroism that echoed through the streets fascinated him. Tales of soldiers marching off to battle ignited a fire within him. Jamie knew he wanted to be part of it.

But there was one major problem—he was 14 years old; the minimum age to enlist in the **Union** Army was 18. His dream of serving his country seemed doomed before it had even begun. However, Jamie wasn't one to give up. With the same determination he'd heard about in those heroic tales, he came up with a plan.

Jamie would become someone else.

He assumed his older cousin's identity—a soldier who'd recently been discharged from the army. Jamie carefully studied his cousin's background, memorizing details of his military service, regiment, and the battles he'd fought. Armed with this fabricated history, Jamie set off to a nearby recruiting station, hoping his youthful appearance wouldn't raise any suspicions.

When he stood before the recruiters, he was ready. He confidently presented himself as his cousin, claiming he'd returned to enlist again. The recruiters, busy and perhaps overwhelmed by the rush of enlistments, didn't ask many questions and accepted him into the Union Army as a drummer boy.

Once in uniform, Jamie was more than just a child with a drum—he was a soldier. He became a vital part of his regiment, earning the respect of older soldiers with his skill and infectious enthusiasm. From the Battle of Antietam to the grueling Siege of Vicksburg, Jamie marched alongside the soldiers, his drumbeat providing a steady rhythm and an unshakable presence on the battlefield.

But throughout all the hardships of war, Jamie kept his secret—his actual age remained hidden from the officers and men around him until after the war, when Jamie's true age was revealed during a medical exam. After the war, Jamie became a symbol of the lengths young people were willing to go to serve their country during the Civil War.

Benny and the Bribe That Beat the Drum

In the middle of the **Civil War**, when drums thundered louder than rules, a pint-sized patriot named Benjamin "Benny" Collins decided he *had* to join the fight. Born in 1849 in a sleepy Pennsylvania town, Benny was raised on bedtime tales of battlefield bravery—and he wasn't about to let something as silly as being underage stop him from becoming a war hero.

Benny cooked up a bold plan. He had squirreled away a few coins from odd jobs around town—shoe-shining, errand-running, and one legendary lawn-mowing escapade involving a goat. That change jingled with purpose in his pocket as he set off one dusky evening toward the local tavern, where recruiters were known to let their guard down with a mug in hand.

Spotting a recruiter with a reputation for being a little... flexible, Benny slid onto the stool beside him and whispered his pitch like a seasoned spy. "Sir, I may be short, but I can drum up a storm. And," he added, slipping the bribe like a magician palming a coin, "I've got this to sweeten the deal."

The recruiter glanced at the boy, the coin, then back again, and then shrugged. "Welcome to the **Union** Army." Benny was in.

With a drum slung over his shoulder and pride in his step, Benny marched off to war. His energy was infectious, his rhythm impeccable, and his secret? Known only to a few trusted comrades. He kept pace through battles like Fredericksburg and Chancellorsville, proving that his courage was anything but child-sized.

But secrets have a shelf life. During the grueling Siege of Petersburg, a surprise inspection unraveled the truth—Benny was barely fourteen. He braced for the worst. But instead of a court-martial, he got a stern talking-to and a sideways smile from the commanding officer. "Well, Collins," he said, "next time, try honesty. But good drumming."

When the war ended, Benny marched home with stories of cannon fire and courage and how a little cash, a big dream, and a whole lot of courage got him into the history books.

The Beat That Bound Three Brothers

During the chaos and cannon fire of the **Civil War**, one Ohio farm boy was determined not to let history march by without him. Meet Thomas "Tom" Anderson, age 15, heart full of grit, and dead set on joining the **Union** Army—even if his birth certificate said otherwise.

Tom wasn't just any underage hopeful; he was the youngest of three fiercely loyal brothers. His older siblings, Robert and William, had already swapped hayfields for battlefields, and Tom wasn't about to be left behind planting potatoes while they charged into glory.

So, in the spring of 1862, with his mind made up, Tom headed to the local recruiting station. He wore his bravest face, puffed out his chest, and presented himself as enlistment material. Of course, the recruiters raised their eyebrows. But Tom had an ace up his sleeve—two of them, actually.

"Those are my brothers," he said, gesturing proudly toward Robert and William. "If they're old enough to fight, I'm old enough to drum."

The officers, caught between military quotas and a healthy dose of brotherly loyalty, gave in. And just like that, Tom Anderson became the regiment's newest—and youngest—drummer boy.

Marching alongside his brothers, Tom quickly became more than just a little sibling tagging along. His drumming kept the unit steady, his spirit kept morale high, and his presence reminded the soldiers that family could stand firm even in the heart of war.

From the muddy mayhem of Shiloh to the thunderous siege at Vicksburg, the Anderson trio stuck together. Tom's drum echoed across battlefields, a steady beat of bravery, brotherhood, and defiance.

When the war finally ended, the three Anderson brothers returned home with medals in their packs and stories in their hearts. But in their quiet Ohio town, it was young Tom's tale that captured imaginations—the bold kid who beat the odds, banged the drum, and stuck with his brothers from start to finish.

A Civil War hero? Absolutely. A family legend? Forever.

The Braveheart with a Drumstick

In the smoky aftermath of the **Civil War**, as the nation stitched itself back together, one young man from Pennsylvania stood out.

Billy Turner, born in 1847, wasn't your typical battlefield hero. At just 15, with cheeks still round from boyhood and a drum slung across his chest, Billy marched into history with the 28th Pennsylvania Volunteer Infantry. While others carried rifles, Billy carried rhythm— and he made every beat count.

On chaotic battlefields, drums delivered signals, orders, and hope. And in 1864, during the brutal Siege of Petersburg, Billy proved just how powerful a drum could be.

As bullets flew and smoke filled the air, Billy didn't hide behind the lines. When his regiment faltered under heavy **Confederate fire**, he sprang into action—dodging gunfire, relaying critical messages between officers, and banging out steady, rallying rhythms to keep the troops from falling apart. Where others saw danger, Billy saw duty.

Soldiers said his drumbeats cut through panic like a knife. Officers called his bravery "unshakable." His regiment called him "the heartbeat of the 28th."

After the war, the stories reached high places. And when medals were handed out, Billy wasn't forgotten. In a ceremony filled with proud veterans and misty-eyed townsfolk, he received the **Medal of Honor** and the rarely awarded **Drummer's Badge**—a special honor reserved for battlefield musicians who had gone *above and beyond*.

Billy's medals weren't just shiny tokens. They were symbols of every kid who answered the call, every drummer who gave the army its pulse, and every act of quiet courage that helped win a war.

And in the little Pennsylvania town where he grew up, Billy Turner's name still marches on—etched into history, one drumbeat at a time.

The Drummer Boy Who Became a Soldier

John Clem, often called **Johnny Shiloh,** was one of the most famous child soldiers of the American Civil War—and he didn't stay a drummer boy for long.

Born in 1851 in Newark, Ohio, John tried to enlist in the 3rd Ohio Infantry at only nine years old but was rejected because of his age. Undeterred, he followed the 22nd Michigan Infantry and was eventually allowed to join as an unofficial drummer boy. The soldiers even chipped in to pay his wages until he was formally enlisted.

John's legend grew during the Battle of Chickamauga in 1863 when he was just **12 years old**. According to popular accounts, a Confederate officer ordered him to surrender during the chaos of battle. Instead, John raised a musket and shot the officer, then ran back to **Union** lines. While some details may have been exaggerated over time, John was promoted to sergeant soon after, making him the **youngest noncommissioned officer** in U.S. Army history.

Confederate forces later captured him but released him in a prisoner exchange. After the war, John didn't leave military life behind. He eventually attended military school, rejoined the army as an officer, and retired in 1915 as a brigadier general—the last Civil War veteran still in active service.

John Clem's story shows how determination and bravery helped a boy with a drum grow into a lifelong leader.

Charles C. Davis:
The Southern Cadence of Courage

Charles C. Davis was one of the best-known **Confederate** drummer boys, remembered for his youth and remarkable devotion to duty during the **Civil War**. Born in Georgia around 1846, Charles enlisted as a drummer in the 1st Georgia Regulars at approximately age 15, though some accounts suggest he may have joined earlier by understating his age.

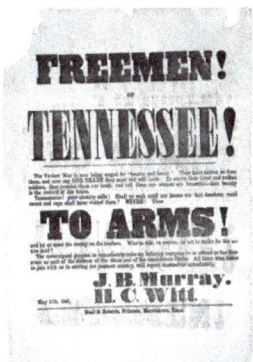

Drummers like Charles were essential to 19th-century warfare, especially in the Confederate ranks. With commands often lost in the chaos of gunfire, the drumbeat kept companies moving, signaling maneuvers, charges, or retreats. Charles was noted for his precise timing and unfailing calm, even during heavy fighting.

During the Peninsula Campaign in 1862, Davis's unit was engaged in the grueling combat of the Seven Days Battles.

> *As shells exploded and men fell around him, Charles remained steadfast, continuing to beat out the necessary commands.*

Officers reportedly pointed him out as a model of composure, noting how his drumming helped maintain unit cohesion when panic threatened to break the line.

Following that campaign, Charles continued to serve through several major engagements, including **Second Manassas** and **Antietam**. While he avoided serious injury, he endured harsh weather, hunger, and the mental strain of life on the front lines, just like the adult soldiers he marched with.

After the war, Charles returned to Georgia, where he became a local figure of admiration. In later years, he participated in veterans' reunions and proudly shared his recollections of the war, especially his time as a drummer boy.

Henry "Dad" Brown

Henry Brown was an African American drummer who served with the **Confederate Army**—a rare and complex role during the Civil War.

Henry's dedication to the drum began in his youth when he joined the 8th South Carolina Infantry as a young boy.

Though not formally enlisted, Henry followed the regiment early in the war, helping with camp duties and learning military drumming from the soldiers. His natural rhythm and quick learning made him an unofficial but essential part of the unit's daily life. By the time the regiment saw action, Henry had earned a place beside the men, beating the calls to rise, drill, eat, and march.

His most remarkable contribution came during the Battle of First Manassas (Bull Run) in 1861. When confusion spread across the lines and many younger boys scattered in panic, Henry remained with the color guard. With shells exploding nearby, he calmly struck out the rhythms needed to reorganize the troops.

Although Henry was never officially listed on Confederate muster rolls due to the limitations and contradictions of the Confederacy's policies toward Black individuals, he was deeply embedded in the unit's history. He continued to serve throughout the war and, after its end, became a fixture in postwar Confederate reunions. He earned his nickname "Dad" Brown as an elderly man who was still proudly beating his drum in parades across South Carolina.

Henry Brown's story reflects the contradictions of the Civil War— how a young African American boy found himself part of the Confederate effort, not through ideology, but through proximity, survival, and personal loyalty to the men he marched beside. His legacy is remembered not just for his drumming but for enduring in a time and place that offered him few choices—and yet making a mark that history could not forget.

Civil War Confederate Blockade Drum and Brass Handle Drumsticks

Each drumstick measures 16 3/4"

The Youngest Medal of Honor Hero

William "Willie" Johnston wasn't just another drummer boy—he became the youngest person ever to receive the Medal of Honor during the Civil War.

Born in 1850 in Morristown, New York, Willie enlisted in the 3rd Vermont Infantry at just 11 years old. His father, who also served in the regiment, helped him join. Willie's job was to beat the drum that set the rhythm for marching, waking, sleeping, and battle formations.

It was a big responsibility for someone so young.

His moment of bravery came during the Peninsula Campaign in 1862, specifically the *Seven Days Battles* near Richmond, Virginia.

After days of hard fighting and retreat, many soldiers—exhausted and discouraged—threw away their equipment to lighten their load.

But not Willie.

He kept his drum, marching the full retreat with it strapped across his chest. When the troops reached safety, he was the only drummer in his division who still had his instrument.

During a review by General George B. McClellan on July 4, Willie was asked to beat the long roll for the parade. His dedication stood out.

Soon after, Willie was **awarded the Medal of Honor**, making him the **youngest recipient in U.S. history** at just 12 years old.

After the war, Willie lived a quiet life, but his name lived on in military history. His story reminds us that courage isn't about size or age— it's about showing up, holding on, and doing your duty when it's hardest.

The Drummer Boy Who Beat the Odds

In the midst of the Civil War, a young boy named **Timothy O'Connor** made his mark on history. At 14 years old, he joined the **Union** Army, eager to serve his country. His slight frame and quick reflexes made him a perfect fit for the role of drummer boy, and soon, he became an essential part of his regiment.

One day, during a skirmish on the outskirts of a small town, Timothy's unit became overwhelmed by Confederate forces. In the chaos of battle, Timothy was separated from his comrades, and before he knew it, he was surrounded and taken as a **prisoner of war**.

Though his captors were initially stern, they soon saw the boy's youth and vulnerability. Many Confederate soldiers were young, and seeing a reflection of their brothers or sons, they offered Timothy water and hardtack, recognizing a common humanity beyond the war.

Timothy found himself in a **Confederate prison camp**, where the conditions were harsh: overcrowded tents, meager rations, and the ever-present threat of disease. Yet, despite these dire circumstances, Timothy's spirit remained unbroken.

As time passed, he noticed his drum tucked away in a corner of the camp. Determined to lift his fellow captives' spirits, Timothy began playing familiar rhythms, the same ones that had guided his fellow soldiers into battle. His drumming brought a sense of unity and camaraderie to the men, even in the most desolate places.

As the war dragged on, Timothy's captors, perhaps softened by his bravery, decided to release him. When he returned to the Union side, his drum still slung over his shoulder, his spirit was **unbroken**.

The Boy Who Beat the System

In a sleepy Illinois town in 1862, 14-year-old Joey Mitchell wasn't dreaming of fishing trips or summer fairs—he was dreaming of battle drums, bayonets, and blue uniforms. With the **Civil War** in full swing, Joey had a fire in his belly and a cause in his heart. The only problem?

He was too young to enlist.

But Joey wasn't one to take "no" for an answer.

Armed with a fountain pen, a sharp mind, and a flair for forgery, Joey crafted a birth certificate that added a couple of years to his age. It wasn't legal, but it was convincing. With his makeshift papers tucked into his coat, he marched into a recruiting station in a neighboring town.

The recruiters glanced at his documents and gave a nod. Just like that, Joey Mitchell was in the **Union** Army.

With a drum slung over his shoulder, Joey joined a regiment bound for the front lines. His rhythm kept the soldiers in step, his spirit lifted weary hearts, and his secret stayed safe—at least for a while.

Joey saw real action, too. At Gettysburg, his steady drumming cut through the chaos. At Petersburg, he was still tapping out commands while cannonballs cracked overhead. He wasn't just a drummer boy—he was *their* drummer boy.

Word of his real age eventually trickled out, but by then, nobody cared. He'd already proven himself ten times over. To his fellow soldiers, he was one of them.

When the war ended, Joey came home not as a runaway kid but as a quiet hero. His parents, shocked at first, couldn't hide their pride. He wasn't the same boy who'd snuck off with fake papers—he was stronger, wiser, and armed with stories no schoolbook could match.

The Drummer Boy Who Raised the Flag

When the cannons fell silent after the **Civil War**, stories of heroism surfaced like embers from a dying fire, but few burned brighter than that of Tommy Reynolds.

Born in 1850 in a quiet Massachusetts town, Tommy was 13 when he marched off to war with a drum strapped to his chest. While most kids his age were worrying about chores and schoolbooks, Tommy was keeping pace with the 11th Massachusetts Infantry, pounding out drumbeats to guide soldiers into battle.

He saw it all—Antietam, Fredericksburg—but it was at Gettysburg where Tommy's name would be etched into history.

Picture this: smoke thick in the air, bullets zipping past, and the Union line teetering on the edge of collapse. Suddenly, the regiment's color bearer goes down, and with him, the American flag tumbles to the blood-soaked ground.

Most would freeze. Tommy *moved*.

He dropped his drum and sprinted toward the fallen banner. Through the chaos, this 13-year-old snatched up the flag, hoisted it high, and charged forward, becoming a beacon in the storm. His bold move sparked a surge in morale. The regiment rallied, pushed back the Confederate advance, and held the line.

Word of Tommy's bravery spread fast. After the war, his tale made headlines. Then came the moment that sealed his legacy: the **Medal of Honor**, draped over his shoulders in a ceremony that brought veterans and civilians to their feet. The youngest soldier in the crowd stood tallest that day.

Rhythm of Resilience

Meet Charles Martin—a real-life hero with rhythm! Born into slavery in Maryland around 1840, Charles didn't wait for freedom to find him—he ran straight toward it. When the **Civil War** broke out, he escaped bondage and made his way to the **Union** Army, ready to fight for a new future.

He joined the legendary 55th Massachusetts Volunteer Infantry, one of the first African American regiments in the Union Army. But Charles didn't carry a rifle—he carried a drum. As a drummer boy, Charles kept his regiment in step and in sync, using rhythm to signal commands and boost morale during the chaos of battle.

One of the most intense moments came during the assault on Fort Wagner in 1863. Amid cannon blasts and flying bullets, Charles's beats cut through the noise—steady, sharp, and fearless. His courage on the battlefield helped shift the tide of war and perceptions of what African Americans could achieve.

Though not every chapter of Charles's life was written down, his legacy thunders on. His drumbeats echoed louder than prejudice, proving that courage, talent, and determination don't care about the color of your skin. Charles Martin wasn't just keeping the beat—he was marching to the rhythm of freedom.

Did you Know?

The contributions of African Americans during the Civil War were vast. While the drummer boy role was more commonly associated with white youths due to societal norms, African Americans served in various capacities, including as soldiers, laborers, and musicians.

The specific stories of black drummer boys from the era may not be as well-documented as those of their white counterparts, but their overall contributions to the war effort were significant and have left an indelible mark on American history.

The Youngest Enlisted Soldier

He picked up a drum at 8 years old and marched into history.

Edward Black holds a tragic and memorable place in **Civil War** history as **the youngest recorded enlisted soldier**, joining the **Union** Army at just **eight years old**.

Born in 1847 in Indianapolis, Indiana, Edward was brought into the 21st Indiana Infantry Regiment by his father, who also served in the unit. Initially a drummer boy, Edward's presence was largely symbolic, representing youthful patriotism and the widespread enthusiasm for the Union cause.

Despite his young age, Edward saw real hardship. He was captured by Confederate forces, endured the conditions of a prisoner of war, and was eventually released in a prisoner exchange. After returning to Union lines, he re-enlisted and continued to serve in a drummer role.

Unlike some drummer boys who lived long lives after the war, Edward's experience left lasting trauma. He struggled with physical and emotional aftereffects, and sadly, he died shortly after his eighteenth birthday.

Today, Edward Black is remembered not only for his youth but also for the sacrifices made by countless children who were swept up in the war. His drum and photograph are preserved in the *Children's Museum of Indianapolis*, offering a powerful reminder of how the Civil War touched even the youngest lives.

Edward Black in uniform, around age 9, with his regulation drum
The Children's Museum of Indianapolis

The Tragedy of Sammy Turner

In the quiet town of Elmridge—far removed from the thunder of battle—lived a boy named Sammy Turner. He was 14, with hands too small for war and a heart too big to ignore it. Driven by a sense of duty, Sammy enlisted in the **Union** Army, his drum slung over his shoulder like a promise he was too young to make.

He wasn't meant for fighting, but his steady rhythm became the beat that gave frightened men something to follow. In the cold gray of an April morning at the Battle of Shiloh, Sammy marched with his regiment into the fire. The air was thick with smoke, torn by cannon blasts and the cries of the wounded. Still, Sammy played. Each beat of his drum defied the violence around him—until it didn't.

No warning. No mercy. A stray bullet cut through the air and found him. His small frame collapsed, and his drum fell silent beside him. At that moment, the rhythm stopped. The soldiers who had marched beside him turned their heads, unable to meet the eyes of a boy too young to die.

Sammy took his final breath on the soil he had marched to defend, surrounded not by family but by war. When the gunfire ceased, a quiet settled over the field, heavier than the smoke. The loss of the regiment's youngest member felt like the loss of something pure, something that shouldn't have been touched by war.

News of his death drifted back to Elmridge. Mothers wept for a boy who wasn't theirs. The church bell tolled, low and slow, as if it too mourned. Sammy's drum was returned, battered and mute, a hollow shell of the voice it once carried.

Sammy Turner became more than a name on a list; he became a sorrow held in the bones of a town that never stopped missing him—a child who gave everything too soon.

The Role of Women in the Military During the Revolutionary and Civil Wars

During the **Revolutionary** and **Civil Wars**, it was rare for girls to serve as drummers in the military. The roles of drummer boys were traditionally filled by young males, often between the ages of **9 and their mid-teens**. At the time, societal expectations and norms kept girls from participating in such roles.

However, there were **exceptional cases** where women disguised themselves as men to serve in the military, and some even took on roles typically reserved for men, including serving as drummers. These women were often motivated by a desire to stay with loved ones, seek adventure, or contribute to the cause they believed in.

But these cases were the exception rather than the rule.

One remarkable example is **Sarah Emma Edmonds**, who served as a nurse and a spy and even fought as a disguised male soldier during the Civil War. Though she wasn't a drummer, her story highlights the risks and challenges women faced when they tried to take on military roles during this time.

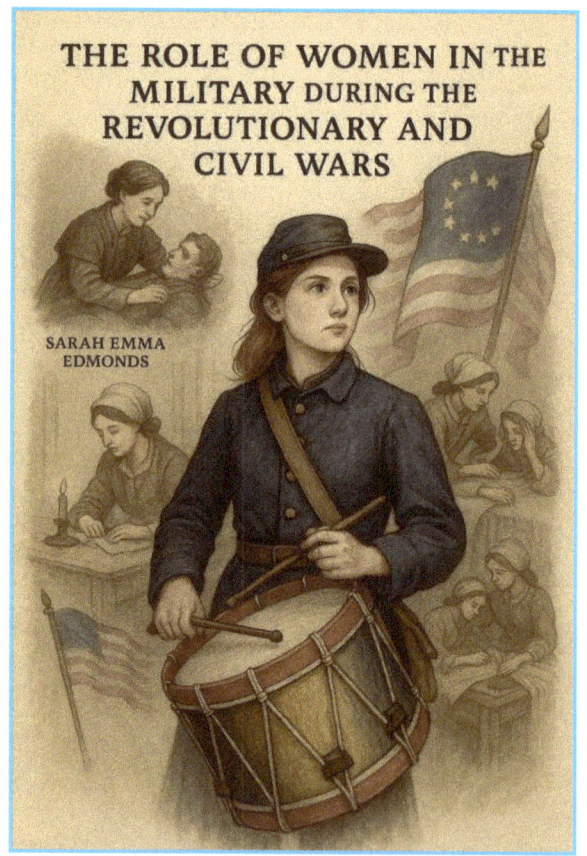

THE ROLE OF WOMEN IN THE MILITARY DURING THE REVOLUTIONARY AND CIVIL WARS

SARAH EMMA EDMONDS

The Beat of a Brave Young Soldier

The image features **Taylor,** a young African American drummer who served in the **78th United States Colored Troops Infantry** during 1864–1865.

In the photograph, Taylor is in uniform, holding his drum.

Why Their Stories Live On

Over the years, many people have written about drummer boys: soldiers who remembered them, authors who admired them, and even the boys themselves. Why? Because these children represented something unforgettable—bravery beyond their years. The memory of that courage still echoes today in books, letters, and memoirs.

Let's look at one of those first-hand accounts now.

The Recollections of a Drummer-Boy **by** Henry Martyn Kieffer offers a window into the life of a young soldier during the American Civil War. First published in the late 19th century, the book follows **Kieffer** as he recounts his time serving as a drummer boy in the Union Army.

Why It's Significant: It gives readers a sense of a boy turned soldier's journey, helping us understand why so many children were drawn to enlist—and what it cost them.

2. Youthful Patriotism The book opens with Harry's longing to join the war. His early reflections capture the romanticism many young boys felt before understanding the horrors of war.

1. Life in Camp and on the March Kieffer describes the daily grind of military life: drills, hunger, and homesickness, revealing the gap between the imagined glory of war and its exhausting reality.

3. Family Conflict Harry's father resists his son's urge to enlist. Eventually, Harry's determination wins out, and he joins as a drummer boy.

4. Exposure to Battle and Loss Harry is a child on the battlefield, witnessing violence, treating the wounded, and losing comrades.

5. Coming of Age Kieffer uses his experiences to show how innocence is lost and character is shaped under extreme circumstances.

Drums Through Time

Military drums have been used for centuries to communicate commands, signal routines, and inspire troops. While this book focuses on Revolutionary and Civil War drummer boys, the role of the drum stretches far beyond one war.

Revolutionary War Drums: These were often handmade and painted with patriotic symbols like eagles, shields, or state names. They had gut snares and calfskin heads, producing a warm, resonant sound. Drummer boys were also used to relay battlefield orders and daily routines.

Civil War Drums: Civil War drums were larger and louder, designed to be heard over cannon fire and marching boots. They usually featured regimental insignia and were worn with a sling across the shoulder. The snare drum became especially important for signaling in battle.

Modern Military Drums: Today, military drums are mostly ceremonial. They're still used in parades and official events, but not for battlefield communication. Modern drums are machine-made with synthetic heads and metal parts, designed for durability and precision.

Revolutionary War Drum

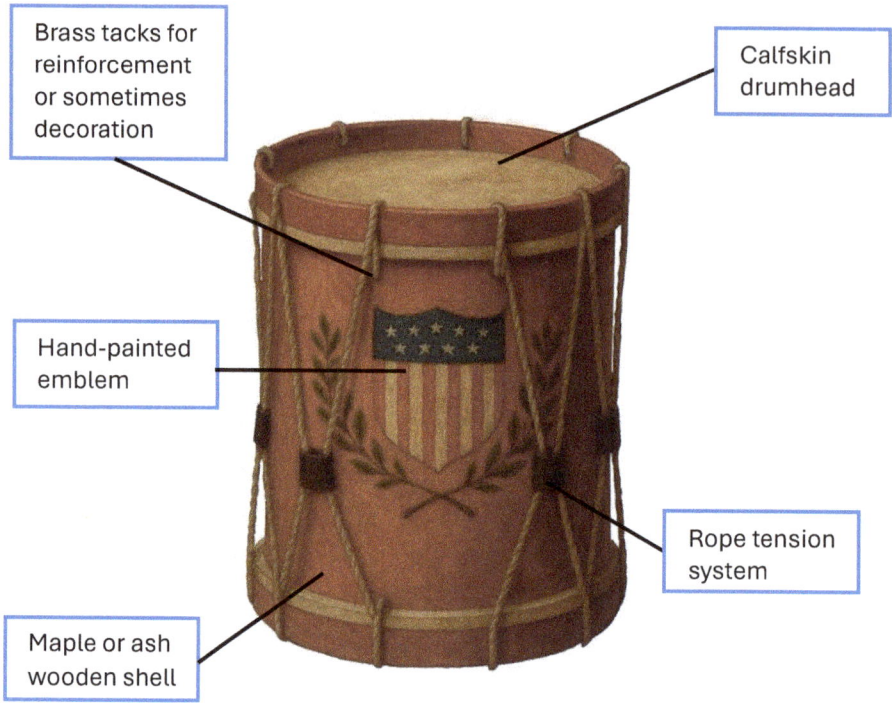

Brass tacks for reinforcement or sometimes decoration

Calfskin drumhead

Hand-painted emblem

Rope tension system

Maple or ash wooden shell

During the American Revolution, drums played a vital role in the army. Soldiers didn't have radios or loudspeakers, so drums and fifes were how leaders gave orders and kept troops moving in sync. The drumbeat told soldiers when to march, attack, retreat, or carry out daily routines.

Revolutionary War drums were usually made of wood with animal skin drumheads and rope tension systems to keep them tight. They were painted with patriotic symbols like eagles, shields, or the thirteen stripes and stars representing the colonies. These bold designs helped build pride and unity among the troops.

Even though drummer boys didn't fight in battle, their job was dangerous. They stood close to the action and had to stay calm under pressure to keep signaling commands. Their steady rhythm helped hold the army together—literally marching to the beat of freedom.

Civil War Side Drum

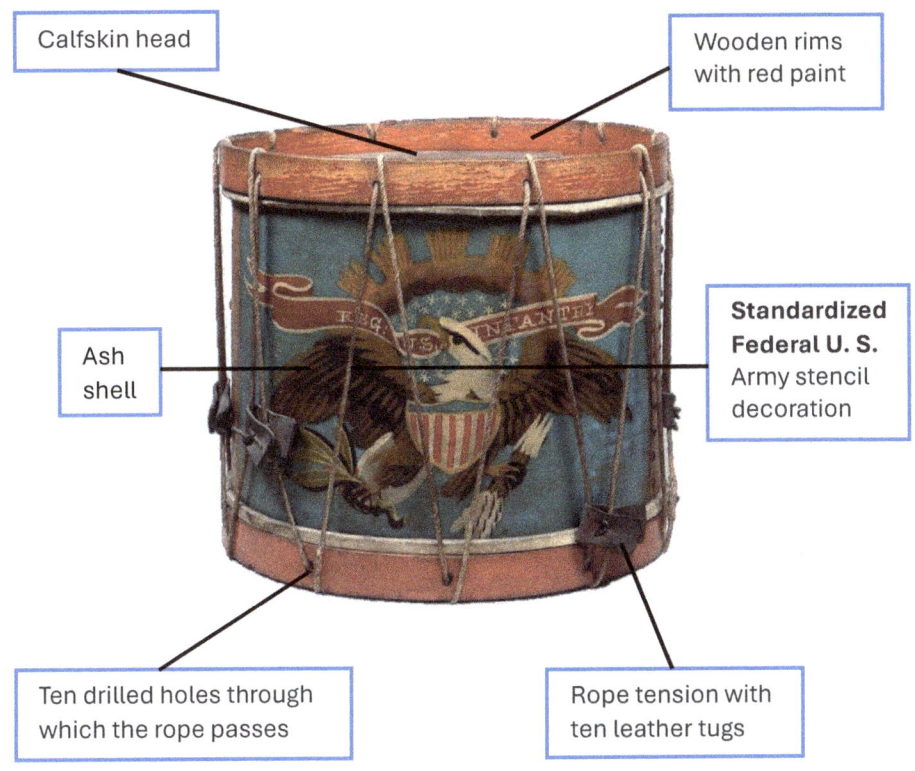

Calfskin head

Wooden rims with red paint

Standardized Federal U. S. Army stencil decoration

Ash shell

Ten drilled holes through which the rope passes

Rope tension with ten leather tugs

What Was a Side Drum?

Side drums were key instruments in the army, especially for infantry. Used since the 1600s in British North America, they helped soldiers stay in step while marching and signaled parts of their daily routine, like when to wake up, eat, drill, or sleep.

The drum hung at a soldier's side (which is how it got its name) and had cords stretched across the bottom that made a buzzing sound when played.

During the Civil War, many Union drums featured painted eagles and blue backgrounds for infantry. Some even had special brass tack patterns—like arrows or circles—that showed who made them.

Modern Military Drum

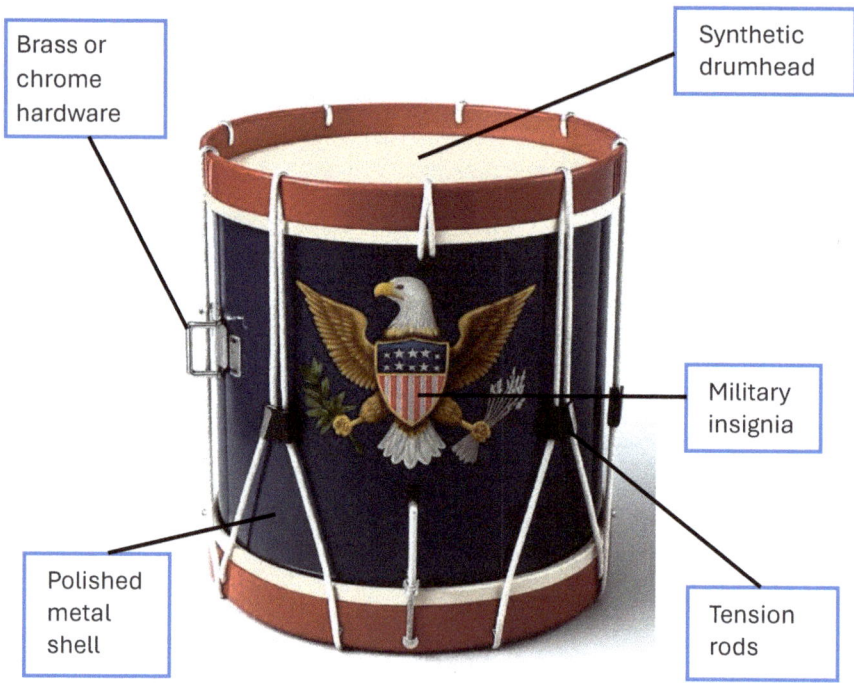

Brass or chrome hardware

Synthetic drumhead

Polished metal shell

Military insignia

Tension rods

Today's ceremonial military drums might look shinier and more polished than their Revolutionary or Civil War counterparts, but their purpose and pride haven't changed. These drums are used in parades, formal ceremonies, and military honors, keeping tradition alive with every beat.

Modern military drums are typically made from durable materials like metal and high-quality plastics, built to last through years of use and travel. Their bold finishes—often in navy blue, red, or black—are paired with detailed insignias, brass fittings, and gleaming rims. The sound is precise and sharp, designed to carry through crowds and open air with clarity.

Though these drums aren't used in battle anymore, they're still a powerful symbol. They connect today's military musicians to centuries of history and remind us that rhythm has always played a role in unity, discipline, and national pride.

A Comparison of Military Drumsticks

Drumsticks have evolved alongside the drums they strike, shaped by the needs of each era. The design of drumsticks reflects changes in warfare, music, and craftsmanship.

1. Revolutionary War Drumsticks

Material: Typically made from solid hardwoods like maple or ash

Shape: Long and narrow with tapered ends; often lacked a rounded tip

Design Purpose: Built to project a sharp, clear tone on rope-tension drums used for field signals in open-air settings

Why Different: These sticks needed to be durable for outdoor use and designed to cut through battlefield noise without amplification

-----

2. Civil War Drumsticks

Material: Also hardwood, but more refined and consistent due to better woodworking tools

Shape: More symmetrical than Revolutionary ones, often with slightly rounded or bulb-shaped tips

Design Purpose: Still used with rope-tension drums, but often matched to standardized military drum models

Why Different: By this period, military music was more organized; drums were used in communication and morale, requiring a blend of durability and tonal clarity

3. Modern-Day Drumsticks

Material: Precision-milled hardwoods (like hickory) or synthetic materials

Shape: Ergonomic handles, balanced weight, and standardized tips (nylon or wood, round or teardrop)

Design Purpose: Engineered for comfort, balance, speed, and compatibility with various drum types (snare, kit, marching)

Why Different: Modern drumsticks are designed for performance versatility and comfort rather than battlefield signaling. The shift from communication to musicality drives the changes

Summary

Historical sticks prioritized volume and endurance in combat.

Modern sticks focus on technique, tone, and playability in musical performance.

Role of the Drum in Communication

On a noisy battlefield, shouting commands wasn't always possible. That's where the **snare drum** came in. Its sharp, clear sound could cut through the chaos of muskets, cannons, and marching boots. **Drummer boys** were trained to play special rhythms—each one with a different meaning.

A **steady beat** might signal soldiers to move forward.
A **fast, sharp rhythm** could mean retreat.

These drum signals helped the army stay organized and move together, even in the middle of a confusing battle.

But it wasn't just the snare drum out there. Armies also used **bass drums** and **fifes** (small flutes). Together, they made a powerful sound that could be heard far and wide. This mix of music helped guide soldiers and boosted their morale, reminding them they were part of something strong and united.

Bass drums and fifes

The Sound of Command:
The Snare Drum in War

During the Revolutionary War and the Civil War, drummer boys typically used a specific type of drum known as the snare drum. The snare drum was well-suited for military use due to its distinctive sound and portability.

Snare Drum Characteristics:

Carrying Straps: To facilitate movement on the battlefield, drummer boys used leather straps to sling the drum over their shoulders.

Material: The drum shell was commonly made of wood, and the drumhead, the surface that is struck to produce sound, was often made of animal skin, usually calfskin. This traditional construction method was used before the widespread availability of synthetic materials.

Did you know? Some drummer boys built their own drums—or helped repair them during camp downtime!

Snare Mechanism: One of the defining features of the snare drum is the presence of wires or gut strings stretched across the bottom drumhead. This snare mechanism produced the distinctive rattling sound associated with snare drums.

Tensioning System: The drumhead was tensioned using ropes or leather straps, allowing the drummer to adjust the drum's pitch by tightening or loosening the tensioning system.

Size: Snare drums used during these historical periods were relatively small and shallow. It made them easy to carry, allowing the drummer boys to move with the troops on the battlefield.

How a Snare Drum Was Made

Creating a snare drum during the Revolutionary and Civil Wars wasn't easy—it took skilled hands, patience, and natural materials. Here's how craftsmen built them using materials available at the time:

__ **1. Drum Shell (The Body)**
Material: Wood like **maple, ash, or cherry**

Process: Thin pieces of wood, called **staves**, were cut and shaped like wedges. These were glued together and clamped to form a **cylinder**—the main body of the drum.

Why it mattered: The type of wood affected the drum's sound—hardwoods gave a louder, clearer tone.

__ **2. Drumhead (The Skin You Hit)**
Material: Animal hides—usually **calfskin or goatskin**

Process: The hide was soaked in water until soft, then stretched tightly across the top and bottom of the shell.

Why it mattered: A tight skin made the drum louder and easier to hear over battle noise.

__ **3. Snare Mechanism (The Rattle Sound)**
Material: Gut strings (from animals) or **metal wires**

Process: Strings were stretched across the bottom drumhead in a crisscross pattern. These vibrated when the drum was hit, making the signature **snappy, rattling sound**.

Why it mattered: The snare helped the drum cut through the noise of battle, making its signals clear.

___ 4. Tensioning System (The Tune-Up)
Material: Ropes or **leather straps**

Process: Ropes were threaded through holes around the shell and then pulled tight to tune the drum.

Why it mattered: Tightening the ropes raised the pitch of the drum. Drummers adjusted this to get just the right sound.

___ 5. Hardware and Carrying Straps
Material: Brass hoops and **leather**

Process: Brass hoops helped keep the drumhead tight, while leather straps were added so the drummer could carry it over the shoulder.

Why it mattered: The drummer needed to move and play at the same time—straps made that possible!

Make Your Own Civil War Style Drum and Drumsticks

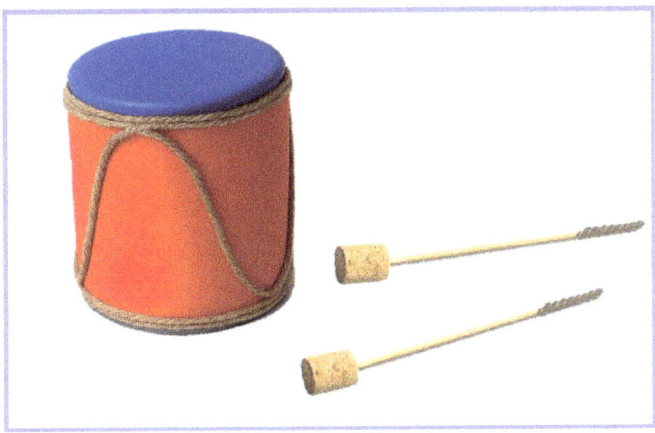

Tools:
Craft knife (adult supervision required)

Ruler

Scissors

Pencil

Pritt Stick (or other paper glue)

PVA glue

Materials Needed

For the Drumsticks:
1 cork

2 wooden skewers

String or twine (approx. 30 cm)

For the Drum:
1 tin with no lid (coffee tin or similar)

1 red sheet of card or thick paper

1 balloon (preferably royal blue)

String or twine

Make the Drumsticks

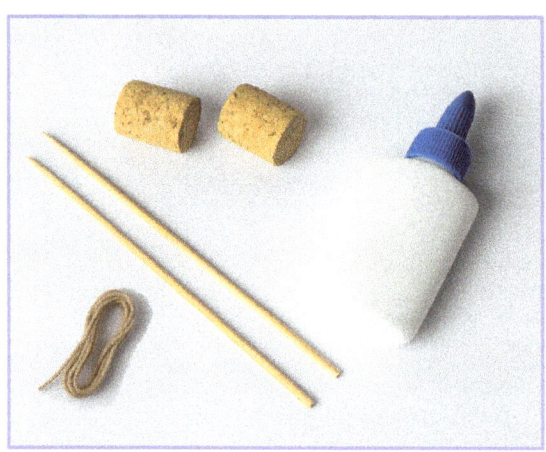

1. **Cut the Cork:**

Use a craft knife to carefully cut the cork in half.

Each half will become the top of one drumstick.

2. **Attach the Corks:**

Take a skewer and gently twist one end into the flat side of a cork half. Remove the skewer, add a small drop of PVA glue inside the hole, then reinsert the skewer. Repeat for the second stick.

3. **Wrap the Handle:**

o Cut a piece of string about 30 cm long.

o Hold one end of the string at the non-corked end of a skewer using your finger.

o With your other hand, tightly wrap the string around the skewer to create a grip. Cover about 3 cm of the stick.

o When done, tie a small knot at the end of the string and trim any extra.

o Repeat for the second stick.

Make the Drum

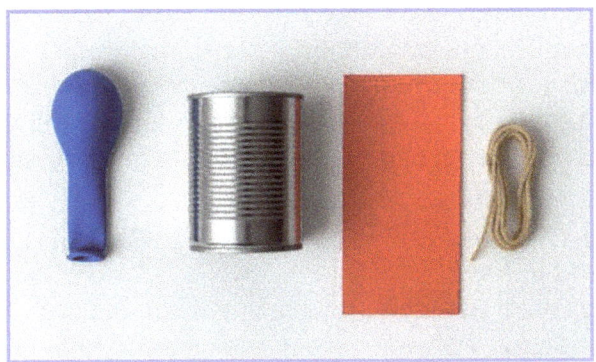

1. **Measure Your Tin:** Use a ruler to measure the height of your tin.

2. **Prepare the Red Card:** Mark the same height on your red card and cut a long strip to wrap around the tin.

3. **Glue the Card:** Cover the back of the card with glue from the Pritt Stick. Wrap it tightly around the outside of the tin, pressing down to secure it.

4. **Stretch the Balloon:** Cut the mouthpiece off the balloon. Stretch the balloon over the open end of the tin so it fits tightly, creating the drum surface.

5. **Decorate with Twine:** o Lay the tin on its side.

o Use PVA glue to draw a wave or zigzag pattern across the red card surface.

o Press a long piece of string or twine onto the glue, following the pattern.

6. **Wrap the Base:**

o Take the remaining twine and wrap it around the bottom edge of the tin several times (about four).

o Secure the end with some glue or a small knot if needed.

How Civil War Drummer Boys Made Their Mark

Not every drummer boy personalized his drum during the Civil War, but many did. For teenage drummers serving in the chaos of battle, their drum wasn't just a tool—it was a symbol of pride, identity, and even survival, and a small act of rebellion in a world full of rules. Even in war, creativity found a way.

Here's how some of them made their drums their own:

1. Names and Initials

Some boys painted their names or initials on the drumhead or shell. It was a simple way to claim their instrument—and maybe to make sure it came back to them after a march or battle.

2. Unit Insignia

Proud of their regiment, some drummers added their unit's emblem or number to their drums. It showed loyalty and let others know who they marched with.

3. Patriotic Art

Flags, eagles, stars, and slogans—symbols of the Union or Confederate causes—sometimes appeared in hand-painted detail, turning each drum into a proud message of allegiance.

4. Creative Designs

Scrolls, vines, and hand-drawn patterns gave drums an artistic personality. For some boys, it was the only canvas they had.

5. Battle Honors

Some marked their drums with the names or dates of battles they'd survived—a personal war record painted on the wood.

6. Quotes and Mottos

A favorite saying, a line from a hymn, or a phrase about bravery or freedom might appear on the drum. These words could serve as motivation—or a reminder of home.

7. Branded Rims

With a heated metal or blade, some boys branded designs into the wooden rims. It was a way to personalize without paint, and the markings lasted.

Decorate Your Drum!

Drummer boys during the Revolutionary and Civil Wars often personalized their drums. Each design told a story about who they were and which side they fought for.

1. **American Flag:** Symbol of Union pride and patriotism during the Civil War

2. **Union Soldier's Cap:** A kepi—commonly worn by Union soldiers

3. **Eagle with Shield:** A powerful American symbol of strength, freedom, and protection

4. **Blue Star and Red "V":** A military insignia, often representing volunteer soldiers

5. **Sailing Ship:** Symbol of naval strength, trade, and adventure; important in both wars

6. **Crossed Rifles with Heart:** Representing bravery, loyalty, and the love soldiers had for their cause

Now it's your turn!

Use paint, markers, or colored pencils to design your own drum art. You can copy one of these ideas—or invent something totally new that shows your spirit. Get creative and make your drum truly yours!

The Revolutionary Drum Beat Code

Drummer boys signaled commands and orders using unique drum patterns, keeping troops in sync. Here are some of the classic patterns and what they meant:

1. **Long Roll:**
   - **Notation:** Rapid alternation between left and right sticks
   - **Meaning:** "Time to move out!" A signal for a general advance, full of urgency

2. **Ratamacue:**
   - **Notation:** Quick succession of three short beats, then a longer one (short-short-short-long)
   - **Meaning:** "Time to turn!" signaled a change in direction or movement

3. **Paradiddle:**
   - **Notation:** Four beats in a specific pattern (e.g., RLRR)
   - **Meaning:** "Listen up!" Used for commands like "Attention" or "Officers' Call."

4. **Flam:**
   - **Notation:** A softer grace note followed by a louder note (big-small)
   - **Meaning:** "Heads up!" emphasized important commands to grab attention

5. **Drag:**
   - **Notation:** Two even beats, followed by a grace note, then an accented third beat (RRLL)
   - **Meaning:** "Shift position!" Signaled changes in formation or movement

6. **Single Stroke Roll:**
   - **Notation:** Alternating single strokes, creating a steady rhythm
   - **Meaning:** "March on!" Used for a consistent cadence or a short rest break

7. **Double Stroke Roll:**
   - **Notation:** Two rapid strokes per hand
   - **Meaning:** "Ready for action!" A faster, more urgent signal to prepare for attack

8. **Three-Stroke Ruff:**
   - **Notation:** Three quick strokes with one hand, followed by a pause
   - **Meaning:** "Attention!" Used to signal a special movement or grab attention

Writing Down Drum Signals: The Secret Drum Code

Drum signals weren't just random beats—they were written down like a secret code! Drummers used special symbols to remember which hand to use (right or left) and how hard or soft to hit the drum. But here's the twist: there wasn't just one way to write them down.

Different armies or instructors might use their own symbols, so the code could vary.

Still, most drummers didn't just rely on paper. They learned by listening, watching, and repeating. Instructors played the rhythms, and drummer boys practiced over and over until the beats were locked in their memory. That way, even if the symbols looked different, they knew exactly what to play when the signal came.

Example: The "Long Roll" Signal

This signal was a fast, steady beat made by quickly switching between right and left hands. On paper, it might look like this:

R L R L R L (with extra marks to show speed and smoothness)

But more importantly, the drummer would **hear** it and know:

"Start a continuous roll—something important is happening!"

No need for fancy music theory—just quick, clear beats!

WRITING DOWN DRUM SIGNALS

THE SECRET DRUM CODE

RRRRRR
LLLLLL

LONG ROLL

The Civil War "Long Roll" Drumming Pattern

The **long roll** was a crucial Civil War drumming pattern drummer boys used to signal troops for immediate action or alert them to urgent situations. Played rapidly and continuously, it conveyed a sense of urgency on the battlefield.

Pattern Breakdown:

- **R** = Right Hand
- **L** = Left Hand
- **D** = Drumbeat

Drumming Pattern:

- Alternating "R" and "L" indicate right or left-hand strikes
- Each "X" represents a drumbeat

R L R L R L R L | R L R L R L R L | R L R L R L R L | R L R L R L R L
D X X X X X X X X | X X X X X X X X | X X X X X X X X | X X X X X X X X

Benefits:

The continuous flow of this pattern created a rapid, intense rhythm, signaling important messages to the troops, like a call to arms or a warning of danger.

This simplified pattern gives a basic representation of the long roll, though its execution may vary based on technique and tradition.

The Single-Stroke Roll

The **single-stroke roll** is a fundamental drumming rudiment consisting of a continuous alternation of single strokes between both hands.

Pattern Breakdown:

- **R** = Right Hand
- **L** = Left Hand
- **D** = Drumbeat

Drumming Pattern:

- Alternating "R" and "L" indicate right or left-hand strikes
- Each "X" represents a drumbeat
- The single stroke roll is characterized by its even, rapid alternation between the right and left hands

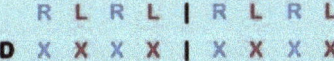

```
R  L  R  L  |  R  L  R  L
D  X  X  X  X  |  X  X  X  X
```

Benefits:

Mastering the single-stroke roll builds a strong foundation for more advanced drumming techniques, enhancing basic coordination and overall drumming ability.

The Three-Stroke Ruff

The **three-stroke ruff** is a fun drum pattern made of three quick hits with one hand followed by one strong hit with the other hand. It adds a cool "lead-in" to your playing—like a mini drumroll before a beat.

Pattern Breakdown:

- **R** = Right Hand
- **L** = Left Hand
- **D** = Drumbeat

Drumming Pattern:

- Alternating "R" and "L" indicate right or left-hand strikes
- Each "X" represents a drumbeat
- Play **three quick, soft hits** with the same hand
- Then play **one loud hit** with the other hand

```
      R  R  R  L  |  R  R  R  L
   D  X  X  X  X  |  X  X  X  X
```

Benefits:

Start slow—keep the first three hits light and even, then finish with a strong, clear beat! It makes your drumming sound **fancy and exciting**.

The Paradiddle

The **paradiddle** is a core drumming rudiment, mixing single and double strokes in a distinct pattern. It's widely used and helps build versatility in drumming.

Pattern Breakdown:

- **R** = Right Hand
- **L** = Left Hand
- **D** = Drumbeat

Drumming Pattern:

- Alternating "R" and "L" indicate right or left-hand strikes
- Each "X" represents a drumbeat

```
    R  L  R  R  |  L  R  L  L
D   X  X  X  X  |  X  X  X  X
```

Benefits:

The paradiddle alternates between single strokes (RL or LR) and double strokes (RR or LL), creating a balanced and controlled rhythm.

Practicing paradiddles enhances coordination and dexterity in both hands, improving overall control and technique.

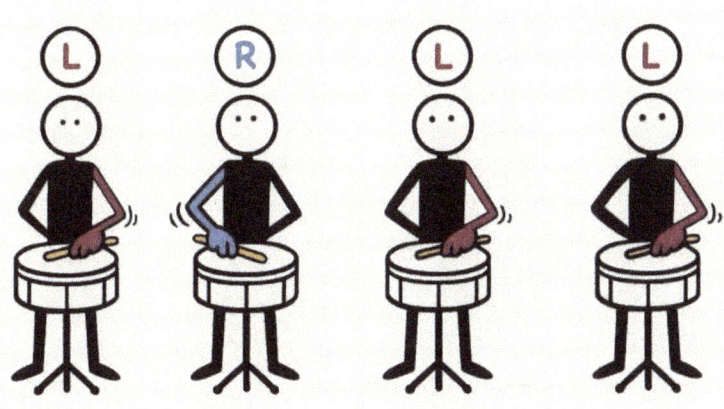

The Ratamacue

The **ratamacue** is a fun, flashy drumming pattern made of three quick notes followed by a special **double hit** called a **drag**. It's great for showing off speed and control!

Pattern Breakdown:

- **R** = Right Hand
- **L** = Left Hand
- **D** = Drumbeat
- **Z** = Drag or Double Stroke

Drumming Pattern:

- Alternating "R" and "L" indicate right or left-hand strikes
- Each "X" represents a drumbeat
- "Z" represents the drag or double stroke, where the stick rebounds for an additional hit.

```
R L R Z | L R L Z
D X X X | X X X X
```

Benefits:

The first three hits (X X X) are single strokes with alternating hands. The last hit (Z) is a drag—a fast double stroke that sounds like a bounce.

The Drag Drum Technique

The **drag** is a drumming technique that adds a quick, fancy sound before a main beat—like a little drum "bounce" before the main strike.

Pattern Breakdown:

- **R** = Right Hand
- **L** = Left Hand
- **D** = Drumbeat

Drumming Pattern:

- Alternating "R" and "L" indicate right or left-hand strikes
- Each "X" represents a drumbeat
- The drag can be executed with either hand
- Keep the first two hits soft and close together
- Then *pop* the last one with confidence to make it stand out

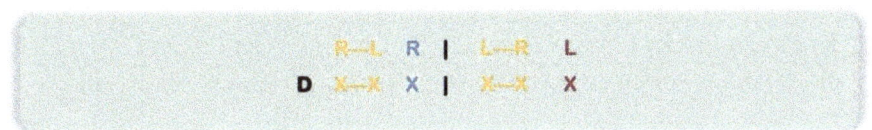

```
        R~L  R  |  L~R  L
    D   X~X  X  |  X~X  X
```

Benefits:

The drag makes your drumming sound more **expressive and exciting**. It's like adding a drum flourish before a big moment.

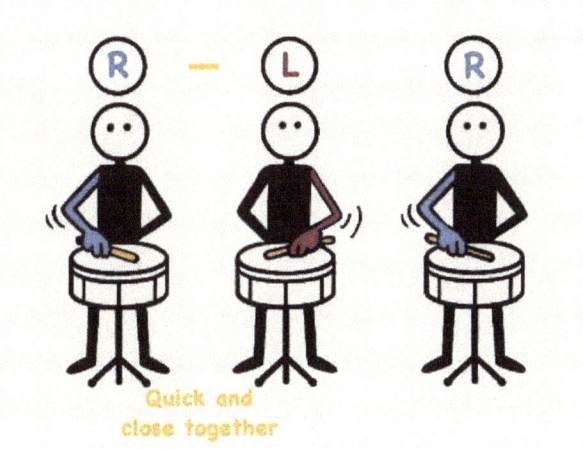

How Drummer Boys Learned
Their Skills in the Civil War

During the Civil War, **drummer boys** weren't just making music— they were an essential part of the army! They learned special drum beats to help send messages, give orders, and keep soldiers moving together. Here's how they trained and practiced to become skilled battlefield drummers:

__ 1. Learning the Rules
Each army had **official rules** for drumming.

Older, experienced drummers showed drummer boys the right beats and patterns used in battle.

__ 2. Mastering the Basics
Single strokes (right-left-right-left) were one of the first things they practiced.

Double strokes (two hits with each hand) helped them play faster and smoother.

__ 3. Learning to Send Signals

Drums weren't just for rhythm—they gave **important commands**.

For example, a **long roll** meant "Get ready—something big is happening!" Other drum patterns told soldiers when to **march, stop, or gather**.

__ 4. Practice in the Field

Drummer boys joined in **training drills**, practicing their beats while soldiers marched or lined up.

They often teamed up with **buglers and fifers** (flute players) to play signals together.

__ 5. Learning Songs and Tunes

Drummers learned special tunes like: o **Reveille** (to wake up the camp)

o **Taps** (for bedtime or honoring fallen soldiers)

o **Marching tunes** to keep everyone in step They practiced these **every day** to keep the beat steady and clear.

__ 6. Lots of Personal Practice

When they weren't on duty, many drummer boys **practiced on their own**, repeating the same patterns over and over.

This helped them get **faster, better, and more confident** with their sticks.

__ 7. Staying Strong in Battle

On the battlefield, things got loud and chaotic.

Drummer boys had to **stay focused** and play clearly, even when they were scared or tired.

Their training helped them **stay calm and communicate fast**.

Drummer boys were more than musicians—they were **messengers, timekeepers, and a steady beat in the heart of the army.** With practice, teamwork, and courage, they played a powerful role in history.

The Mystery of the Civil War Drum

This photograph features a Civil War drum displayed at the Soldiers and Sailors National Military Museum and Memorial in Pittsburgh, Pennsylvania.

However, there is no specific information about its original owner. While it's plausible that a drummer boy used the drum— given the common practice of employing young drummers during the Civil War—there is no documented evidence confirming this drum's association with a drummer boy.

What Happened After?
Life Beyond the Drum

Drummer boys didn't stay boys forever. After the last battles were fought and the drums fell silent, these young veterans returned home, often changed by what they'd seen and done. Many carried the memories of war for the rest of their lives, but they also carried skills, strength, and stories that helped shape who they became.

Some used their musical talents to become professional musicians or bandleaders. Others became teachers, craftsmen, ministers, or writers, using their experiences to inspire and educate future generations. A few wrote memoirs or gave speeches at veterans' events, ensuring the legacy of drummer boys would never be forgotten.

Mini-Biographies:

✦ Sammy Turner (page 26)
Known for his sharp rhythm and spirit on the battlefield, Sammy returned home and dedicated his life to mentoring young musicians. He became a beloved band instructor and community leader.

✦ William "Willie" Johnston (page 34)
Awarded the Medal of Honor at age 13, Willie became a symbol of bravery. He later lived a quiet life, known for his humility and service.

✦ Henry Martyn Kieffer (page 43)
After serving in the Union Army, Kieffer became a minister and author. His book, *The Recollections of a Drummer-Boy*, gave readers a vivid picture of wartime youth.

LIFE BEYOND THE DRUM

BRAVERY AT 13
Willie Johnston

TEACHER OF TUNES
Sammy Turner

VOICE OF MEMORY
Henry Kieffer

These boys grew into men whose lives were forever shaped by the rhythm of war. Their legacy lives on—in history books, music, and the values of courage, resilience, and service.

The Last Beat of the Drum

As the echoes of the drums faded into history, the role of the drummer boy became a symbol of courage, resilience, and the spirit of a nation in the midst of war. These young hearts, who marched to the rhythm of duty and sacrifice, are long gone, but their legacy endures in the stories they left behind.

Today, the drums are silent, but the memories of those who played them remind us of the price of freedom, the value of perseverance, and the hope that even the youngest among us can make a lasting impact.

The beat may have stopped, but the story of the drummer boy lives on, not just in history but in each of us, reminding us that we all have a role to play in shaping the future.

The Legacy of Military Drumming

Military drumming has a rich history that transcends the Revolutionary and Civil Wars. Over time, drum signals evolved to meet the needs of later wars, from the World Wars to modern-day conflicts. The patterns once used to command troops on the battlefield have shaped modern military communication and even inspired musical rhythms in today's marching bands and popular music. The legacy of these drumbeats lives on, influencing military practices and cultural expressions worldwide.

As you close the pages of this first book, you've just begun to uncover the stories of young heroes who shaped the course of history. But the journey doesn't end here. The next book in *The Teen Warrior Series* will take you deeper into the heart of war, where you'll meet new young warriors who fought with everything they had to secure freedom. Get ready for more bravery, more tough choices, and more heroes who are just like you.

What will you do when faced with a world at war? The next chapter of their story is waiting. Are you ready to answer the call?

www.ingramcontent.com/pod-product-compliance
Lightning Source LLC
Chambersburg PA
CBHW051237120626
46547CB00013B/1681